Last Man

4

The Show

Balak + Sanlaville + Vivès

New York

OKAY, LET'S RESET LIGHTS!
SWITCH WARDROBE TO OUTFIT 4.
TOMIE, PLEASE STAY ON SET.
PAT, QUICK TOUCH-UP ON MAKEUP, PLEASE?
OKAY, JIP.
UM...
MISS KATANA?
FOR THE TOUCH-UP–
YOU GOT A LIGHT?
HUH?
OH NO, I DON'T... SORRY.

WHERE'D SHE GO?
SHE WENT FOR A SMOKE.
WHERE?
I DON'T KNOW, JIP.
GODDAMN IT! SHE'S SUCH A PAIN IN THE ASS.
ALL GOOD, GUYS...
SHE'S IN THE EAST WING.
OKAY, TWO-MINUTE BREAK.
NO SMOK

TIP
TIP
TIP
TIP
TIP.
Great day
work's amaz

TOMIE, BABE!
SORRY TO RUSH, BUT WE'RE READY FOR YOU ON SET.
!
OH.
OKAY.
UM...
TOMIE NEEDS A BREATHER, JIP.
BUT, DAMN— WE'RE ALREADY RUNNING LATE.
JUST FIVE MINUTES.
SURE, OKAY, WE CAN CHECK LIGHTS AGAIN...BUT FIVE MINUTES—NO MORE!

MY BROTHER AND I NEVER GOT ALONG. BUT THAT FRANCIS...
WELL, HE WAS A BIT LIKE YOUR ADRIAN.
MY BROTHER USED TO SAY WE HAD MORE OR LESS THE SAME JOB...
HE KNEW IT DROVE ME NUTS.
YES, I MEANT TO ASK...
WHAT IS IT THAT YOU DO HERE? THIS BUILDING'S HUGE!
!
YOU DON'T KNOW ZOTIS INC.?
FRANCIS SAID YOU WEREN'T FROM AROUND HERE, BUT STILL...
WHAT DO YOU DO, SWEETIE?
I'M A BAKER.
THAT'S NICE. SO, YOU SELL MUFFINS...
Zotis INC.

WELL, I SELL DREAMS.

HOW SWEET. SAY THANK YOU, ADRIAN.

WHOA...

FIGHT FUNERAL
FIST CUP
AH.
SO, *THAT'S* MORE UP HIS ALLEY.

WE ALSO RUN THE FIGHT FIST FUNERAL CUP.
THE GREATEST BOXERS IN THE WORLD COMPETE. I CAN GET YOU TICKETS. IT'S A GREAT THING TO SEE WHILE YOU'RE IN TOWN.

"FIGHT FIST"?
OH!

THEN MAYBE YOU KNOW...
HM?
JUST A SEC–

SCANDAL!
Final match ends in shame: Aldana banned from league for life
DO YOU KNOW ABOUT THIS?
...AND WHERE I COULD FIND THIS RICHARD ALDANA?
LISTEN, IT'S BETTER TO TALK TOMORROW.
I CALLED FOR A CAR TO DRIVE YOU TO YOUR HOTEL.
OKAY, THANKS, BUT–
AND IF THERE'S ANYTHING ELSE I CAN DO, FEEL FREE TO ASK.
THANK YOU.

BYE.
ZOTIS INC
HEY!

HMM...
TIP
TIP

CHECK OUT THE CAR! IT'S LIKE THAT ONE IN NILLIPOLIS.

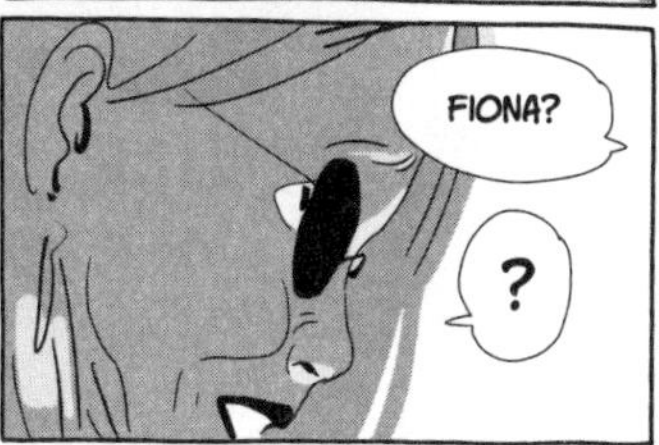
FIONA?
?

TOMIE?
WHY ARE YOU WANDERING THE HALLS IN YOUR BATHROBE? YOU'LL-
WHO WAS THAT?
WHA-
WHO?
THAT GIRL WITH THE KID- WHO WAS SHE?
N...NOBODY... HEY!
GRAB!
Milo
looking for
R.ALDANA

TOMIE!
MISS KATANA!
STOP!
TAC
TAC
TAC

HEY, WAIT!
TOMIE!
MISS KATANA, TWO MINUTES!
FREAKING PAPARAZZI...
HONK!
HONK!
WHAT'S GOING ON?
SIT DOWN, ADRIAN.

TOMIE, OVER HERE!
BLAM!
MOVE IT!
GET THE HELL OUTTA HERE!
I WANT TO SEE MILO!
NOW!
looking for R.ALDANA
10:22
BEEP!
BEEP BEEP!
WHAT A COINCIDENCE!

SO TELL ME—
HOW DO YOU FIND
THE SCOTCH? I SAVED
THE BOTTLE FOR JUST
THIS OCCASION.

OH, RICHARD, RICHARD...
I DIG YOUR STYLE- YOU KNOW THAT?
H, IF YOU PLEASE...
HAND HIM HIS "BREWSKI" AND LEAVE US.
WE HAVE A FEW THINGS TO DISCUSS.
YOU GOT IT.

I TRUST YOUR LITTLE TRIP DID YOU SOME GOOD?
I GOTTA ADMIT, I DIDN'T MISS THE PAXTOWN AIR, BUT YOU KNOW ME... I MADE SOME FRIENDS...
SO H SAID.
TO BE HONEST, I NEVER IMAGINED YOU'D BE TAKEN IN BY THOSE NILLIPOLIS LOSERS!
OKAY, YEAH, I MIGHT'VE UNDERESTIMATED THEM. I RAN INTO A LOT OF DIRTY GUYS, BUT DON'T YOU WORRY, MILO...
YOU STILL TOP 'EM ALL!
HMPF!

WE DRAG YOU OUT OF THE NILLIPOLIS JAIL...
...YOU COME BACK BROKE, DESPITE OUR AGREEMENT...
...AND NOW YOU INSULT ME IN MY OWN HOME...
I'M AN EASYGOING GUY, RICHARD, BUT THAT HURT!
ME AND ALL THE LEAGUE'S FANS.
BUT YOU KNOW WHAT?
IT'S OKAY! I'LL WIPE THE SLATE CLEAN.
AND AS FOR THE DEBT...

DON'T WORRY ABOUT IT.
LET ME TELL YOU SOMETHING, RICHARD...
THE REASON YOU'RE HERE COMFORTABLY SIPPING THAT BEER IS BECAUSE I HAVE PLANS FOR YOU. CONSIDER YOURSELF LUCKY, MY FRIEND.
YOU COULD BE AT THE BOTTOM OF PAXTOWN BAY RIGHT NOW, WITH PIRANHAS GNAWING ON YOUR BALLS!

PAXTOWN STADIUM...
YOU CAN DROP US HERE, SIR.

CLICK!
HEY!
WHAT THE-
CLACK
CLACK!
MY ORDERS
WERE TO DRIVE
YOU TO THE
HOTEL!
BLAM!
SHRiiii
SORRY, BUT
THE HOTEL'S
GONNA HAVE
TO WAIT.

WHERE ARE WE GOING?

TO SEE RICHARD?

STEAK

ANOTHER SHOOTING?!
BEAT IT, MIDGET!
WAS MILO ZOTIS BEHIND IT?
MILO ZOTIS...
GET OUTTA HERE!
WHO'S THE VICTIM? ANY GANG TIES?
EXCUSE ME...

SIR?...
LET GO OF ME!
DID YOU SAY "MILO ZOTIS"?

WHAT?!
CAN'T YOU SEE I'M BUSY?

?

I'VE SEEN THAT BEFORE.
THAT DESIGN...

PETER VERKAIK, INDEPENDENT JOURNALIST...
DO YOU HAVE A MINUTE?
I SAID GET THE HELL OUT!

I THOUGHT ZOTIS HAD ALDANA KILLED...
BUT YOU'RE SAYING HE'S ALIVE?... COULD BE...
WHAT'S WITH THAT LION'S HEAD, THOUGH?
ARE YOU PART OF SOME SECRET SOCIETY?
YOU COULD SAY THAT...
BUT TELL ME—WHAT HAPPENED DURING RICHARD'S FIGHT?
THE FINAL? WELL, ALDANA WAS AT HIS PEAK! HE WAS GOING FOR HIS THIRD STRAIGHT TITLE. HE WAS THE FACE OF A NEW GENERATION OF BOXERS.
FANS, SPONSORS, NOBODY COULD GET ENOUGH.
HEY, KID, GIMME A DOLLAR!

THEY ADORED HIM.
AND THEN THERE WAS HIS PARTNER, DUKE DIAMONDS. EVER SINCE THE LEAGUE PAIRED THEM UP, THEY'D BEEN UNSTOPPABLE.
AGAIN, THEY WERE BY FAR THAT YEAR'S LEADING CONTENDERS.

THEIR CHALLENGERS DIDN'T STAND A CHANCE. IF ALDANA HADN'T FLIPPED, THERE'S NO WAY THEY WOULD'VE WON THAT CUP.
BANUS
AND GIVEN THE ANGER OF BOTH THE FANS AND THE LEAGUE...

...HE WAS EXPELLED. APPARENTLY HE GOT INVOLVED IN UNDERGROUND BOXING, BUT ZOTIS MADE HIM DISAPPEAR FAST!
KID... MY FIX...
NEED MY FIX.

ALDANA WAS DEFINITELY ASKING FOR IT.

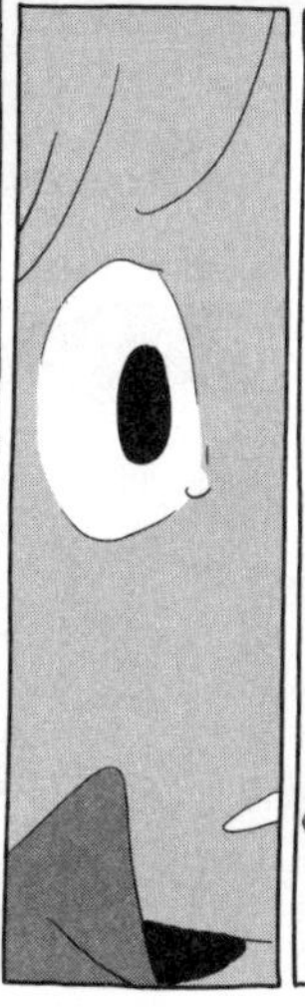

BUT WHAT HAPPENED EXACTLY? IN THAT FIGHT?
HERE WE ARE!

PAXTOWN STADIUM.
OR RATHER...
ZOTIS STADIUM.

HEADQUARTERS OF ORGANIZED CRIME.

I HAVE PROOF OF EVERYTHING. ONE DAY I'LL BRING IT TO LIGHT.

HOLD ON– I'LL SHOW YOU...

I TOOK THIS DURING THE FINAL.

I CAN'T SEE A THING.
OKAY, SO THERE WASN'T MUCH LIGHT. AND MY FINGER'S THERE BECAUSE SOMEONE SHOVED ME...

ONE DAY THEY'LL PAY FOR THEIR CRIMES...

COME ON...
WE'RE GOING TO CRUCIFY THEM!

PRICE
BANUS
FIST

AH, RICHARD! YOUR FACE HAS BEEN POUNDED SO MANY TIMES, I BET YOU DON'T FEEL MUCH OF ANYTHING.

LOOK AT WHAT YOU'VE BECOME...

SOME PATHETIC HAS-BEEN...

IF YOU COULD WRAP THIS UP, MILO, WE'D ALL BE BETTER OFF.

WRAP IT UP?
WE'RE NOT EVEN CLOSE TO WRAPPING IT UP.
LIKE I SAID, I'VE GOT PLANS FOR YOU.

THIS YEAR'S FIGHT FIST FUNERAL CUP...
YOU'RE IN IT.

WHAT?

I SUGGEST YOU TELL YOUR GOONS TO PUT A BULLET IN MY HEAD.

IT'D SAVE US TIME...
...AND KEEP ME FROM GETTING MIXED UP AGAIN IN YOUR GODDAMN CIRCUS.

YOU ASSHOLE. YOU'RE GONNA—
HOLD IT!
OH, RICHARD...
HEH HEH...
HA HA HA HA!!!
YOU STAY DOWN.
A BULLET IN THE HEAD, YOU SAY?
YOU KNOW, RICHARD...I'VE ALWAYS WONDERED IF YOUR BIG MOUTH WAS ALL BRAVADO OR A REAL DEATH WISH.
MILO...

NOT ONLY ARE YOU FIGHTING IN THE FFFC, RICHARD, BUT YOU'RE GOING TO BEG ME FOR IT.

3...

HA! YOU JUST CAN'T HELP YOURSELF, CAN YOU?
TSHH
MMMMMM
YEAH, NICK, NOT NOW...
MMMMMM
WHAT?
BEG ME, RICHARD—BEG...
BOSS...
I'M BUSY, MIGUEL.
SORRY, BUT THERE'RE PEOPLE IN THE LOBBY ASKING TO SEE YOU ABOUT ALDANA.
A DWARF WITH GLASSES, AND ALSO...
...SOME BLONDE CHICK WITH A KID.
!

LET... ME... SEE...
BRING THE GIRL AND KID.
RIGHT UP HERE.
C'MON, RICHARD, FESS UP!
WHAT?
WHAT DID YOU GET UP TO THIS TIME?
NO, DON'T TELL ME...
YOU KNOCKED HER UP AND 'SPLIT'?

NO, WAIT...
YOU TOLD HER SWEET NOTHINGS AND TOOK OFF WITH HER CASH.
THE PUBLIC'S GOT A RIGHT TO BE INFORMED!
STAY BEHIND THE DOOR.
THE TRUTH WILL COME OUT, AND YOU CAN'T–
YOU'RE GONNA GET SLAPPED.
I HAVE HERE–
SEE THIS HAND?
WE'RE HERE TO SEE MR. ZOTIS, AND YOU CAN'T–
MMMMM
YEAH.
MMMMM
RIGHT.
THE KID AND THE GIRL CAN GO UP.
AH!
NOT YOU, MR. TOURIST. YOU'RE GOING HOME.
?
SHHCLAC!
BUT–

MR. ZOTIS WILL SEE YOU.
I HAVE A FEELING OUR LITTLE FAMILY REUNION WILL PROVE QUITE MOVING.
ISN'T THAT RIGHT, RICHARD?
HMM? NOTHING TO SAY ANYMORE?
MOM... THESE STAIRS GO UP BY THEMSELVES!

GUESTS OF MILO'S.
OKAY.
KNOCK KNOCK

HEY, BOSS! THEY'RE HERE!

SHOW THEM IN.

MY DEAR FRIENDS— WELCOME!
IT'S A PLEASURE TO MEET YOU! I'M MILO ZOTIS.

RICHARD!
RICHARD, IS THAT YOU?
WELL, RICHARD, AREN'T YOU GOING TO SAY HELLO?

RICHARD...
LOOK AT ME!
I...
MILO!

WHAT'S THE STORY WITH-
!!!

RICHARD! YOU DAMN BASTARD!
TURN AROUND!
TOMIE.
MY, YOU'RE ADORABLE. AND YOU SURE HAVE A FLAIR FOR THE DRAMATIC.
BUT, PLEASE...
SHUT UP.

...

NOW, WHERE WERE WE?

CARE TO CLUE US IN, RICHARD?
HMM? NOTHING?

AND YOU'RE USUALLY SUCH A CHATTERBOX...

SEEMS TO ME
YOU OWE YOUR WIFE
AN EXPLANATION,
PERHAPS?
EX-WIFE.

GOD,
I'M SUCH AN
AN IDIOT...

I DON'T KNOW ABOUT YOU GUYS, BUT ME...I'M LOVING THIS.

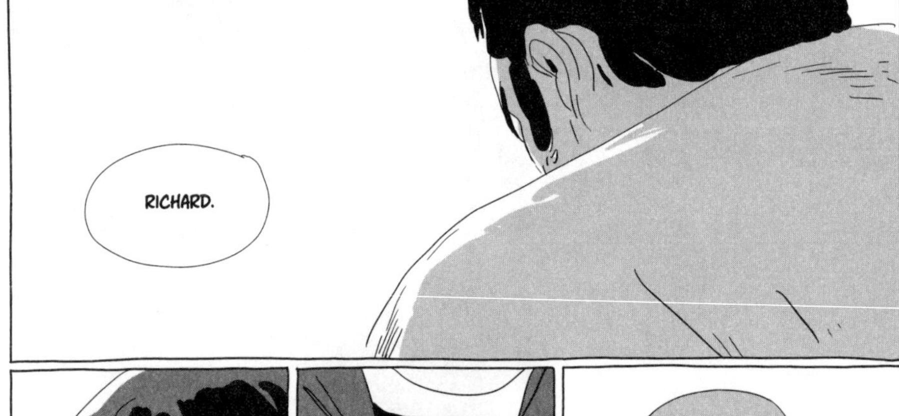

WELL, MOM BOUGHT IT FOR ME...

IT TALKS ABOUT THE VALLEY... I'VE ALREADY GOTTEN THIS FAR. THAT'S THE GREAT KNIGHT AND THIS IS THE RIFT.

WE TOOK A BOAT TO GET HERE! WE HAD TO LEAVE BEHIND THE BIKES.

ADRIAN.

AND OH YEAH—THIS IS THE GREAT LION, AND THERE ARE EVEN SOME FIGHTERS. HANG ON...
ADRIAN, STOP.
AND IN NILLIPOLIS, WE FOUND THE CUP...
...
HEY, KID! YOU A FRIEND OF RICHARD'S?
YEAH. WE WON THE ROYAL CUP TOGETHER.
THE ROYAL CUP?
UH-HUH. AND WE WERE UP AGAINST CRISTO CANYON IN THE FINALS, AND RICHARD BEAT HIM WITH ONE PUNCH!

HEH HEH... PARTNERS, HUH? IS THAT SO, RICHARD?
MILO!
WHAT'S YOUR NAME, KID?
ADRIAN VELBA.

ADRIAN VELBA! SOUNDS LIKE THE NAME OF A CHAMP! DID YOU KNOW WE HAD AN ADRIAN WHO WON THE FFFC? SOME TWENTY YEARS AGO.
WHAT'S THE FFFC?
THE FIGHT FIST FUNERAL CUP. IT'S THE TOURNAMENT I RUN.

RICHARD! YOU HEAR THAT? THEY HAVE A TOURNAMENT! LET'S PARTNER UP!
ADRIAN...

YEAH, RICHARD, THAT'S A GREAT IDEA!
WEREN'T YOU JUST ASKING ABOUT A PARTNER?

CUT THE CRAP, MILO.
THIS ISN'T A GAME. LEAVE THE KID OUT OF IT.

COME ON, RICHARD. YOU GUYS WON THE ROYAL FLUSH OR WHATEVER...
YOU MAKE A GREAT TEAM!
MILO, YOU BASTARD...
STOP IT!
YOU KNOW WHAT, ADRIAN? I'M GONNA SIGN YOU UP WITH RICHARD. IT'LL BE–
MILO!
I TOLD YOU TO LEAVE HIM OUT OF IT!
HE'S JUST A KID...HE CAN'T FIGHT. IT'S A JOKE!
I'M YOUR PROBLEM, NOT HIM!
BUT...
?

WHY WOULD YOU SAY THAT...
...THAT I DON'T KNOW HOW TO FIGHT?
ADRIAN, IT'S FOR YOUR OWN-
THAT'S ENOUGH!
SO MY SON'S NOT GOOD ENOUGH FOR THE GREAT RICHARD ALDANA?
YOU DON'T NEED HIM ANYMORE...
...SO YOU JUST DUMP HIM?

MARIANNE, FOR GOD'S SAKE!
THIS ISN'T THE TIME!

REMEMBER WHAT I TOLD YOU IN THE VALLEY, RICHARD?
THAT IF YOU HURT ADRIAN...

...THERE WON'T BE A PLACE IN THE WORLD WHERE YOU CAN HIDE.

MR. ZOTIS, IS IT?
YES?
YOU'RE ENTERING ME AND MY SON IN THAT TOURNAMENT OF YOURS.

...
REALLY?
HMM...

DAMN IT, MARIANNE! HAVE YOU GONE NUTS?
THIS ISN'T A JOKE—WE'RE NOT IN SOME BACKWATER HOLE.
FWAP!
DON'T YOU.
TOUCH. ME.

HEE HEE...
THIS IS MOST UNEXPECTED.
A SPURNED WOMAN AND HER SON...
READY TO DO BATTLE.

I LOVE IT!
IT'S GENIUS!

THIS CAN'T BE REAL!!!

H, MAKE IT HAPPEN! WE'VE GOT A GOLD MINE HERE.
OKAY.
NO, WAIT, EVEN BETTER...

TOMIE, SWEETHEART...
HUH?
YOU'LL BE LOOKING AFTER OUR TWO GUESTS.
WHAT?
...
NO, THIS CAN'T-
AND I'LL KEEP RICHARD RIGHT HERE WITH ME.
TAKE GOOD CARE OF THEM. AND NO SNIFFING THAT STUFF OF YOURS IN FRONT OF THE KID.
SHUT UP, MILO.
TOMIE...
BEAUTIFUL! MY FRIENDS, THIS YEAR'S FFFC...

...WILL BE UNFORGETTABLE!
WAIT!
TOMIE!

YOU WERE JOKING BACK THERE, RIGHT?
...ABOUT PUTTING YOUR KID IN THE FFFC.
DO WHATEVER YOU WANT, BUT HERE'S SOME ADVICE ON ALDANA: FORGET ABOUT HIM, LIKE I DID.

HE'S NOT WORTH IT.
VOOOM
KLANG!
GREAT!
MIKE, GO RUN THAT TO LEGAL.
R. Aldana

YOU SEE, RICHARD, I KNEW WE'D FIND A WAY TO RESOLVE OUR ISSUES.
THOSE TWO SURE MAKE FOR A NICE GIFT—THANKS!

SCREW YOU, MILO!
HA HA! IF I HAD A DOLLAR FOR EVERY TIME YOU'VE INSULTED ME...
BUT SERIOUSLY, NOW...NO ONE WANTS ANYTHING TO DO WITH YOU AFTER THAT LITTLE MISHAP OF YOURS...

YOU EVEN HAD TO TEAM UP WITH A CHILD...
A CHILD NOW PARTNERS WITH HIS MOM.
SO THE QUESTION IS: WHO CAN TAKE DUKE'S PLACE?

DON'T YOU DARE SAY HIS NAME!
I'LL SAY WHATEVER THE HELL I WANT. MIGUEL?

THWACK
THOSE REFLEXES NEED WORK, BIG GUY...
I ASSUMED NO ONE COULD EVER BE CRAZY ENOUGH TO FIGHT BESIDE YOU.
ANYWAY, AS I WAS SAYING...
BUT IT TURNS OUT I WAS WRONG!
THERE'S SOMEONE JUST DYING TO BE YOUR PARTNER.
LOOK THERE!
H BROUGHT HIM BACK FROM NILLIPOLIS...

PAK
PAK
PAK
PAK
PAK
PAK
PAK!

WAAAM!

SHWW..
ADRIAN...
SOMETIMES GROWN-UPS SAY THINGS THEY DON'T MEAN.
YOU'RE A GREAT FIGHTER, TRUST ME.

SO DON'T LET THAT GET YOU DOWN.
GOT IT?
MOM?
HMM?
IS IT TRUE WE'RE GONNA DO THE TOURNAMENT TOGETHER?
YES, IF YOU DON'T MIND HAVING YOUR OLD MOM AS A PARTNER.
YOU'RE NOT OLD.
THANKS, SWEETIE.
WAIT, I WANNA SHOW YOU SOMETHING.
IN THE DESERT, YOU DID A SUMMONING...
AND IT SAYS HERE...

"STRONGER AND MORE DEVASTATING..."
"...THE KNIGHT'S SUMMONING DESTROYS ALL HIS OPPONENTS."
"BUT IT CAN ONLY BE PERFORMED..."
ACE-OFF UPON THE MONSTER'S RETURN
THE KNIGHT'S SUMMONING
"...BY A KNIGHT OF THE ROYAL GUARD. THUS THE–"
WAIT A SEC... WHAT KIND OF BOOK IS THIS?
MOM, THAT WASN'T THE SCHOOL-OF-HEAVENS SUMMONING YOU DID IN THE DESERT...
SO WHAT WAS IT?
WHEN I WAS YOUNGER, I KNEW SOME OF THE NAMES. NOW I DON'T REMEMBER THEM ANYMORE.
THAT'S NOT TRUE. YOU DO!

I SAID I'D FORGOTTEN THEIR *NAMES*, NOT HOW TO DO THEM...
WE CAN PRACTICE TOMORROW MORNING, BEFORE THE TOURNAMENT.

KNOCK KNOCK
MRS. VELBA, PARDON ME FOR INTERRUPTING...
I WANTED TO LET YOU KNOW DINNER IS SERVED.

THANK YOU, THAT'S VERY KIND. WE'LL BE THERE SOON.
TAKE YOUR TIME.

CLICK

KNOCK
KNOCK
MISS KATANA...

ARE YOU SURE YOU DON'T WANT TO HAVE DINNER WITH YOUR GUESTS?
MISS KATANA... PLEASE BE REASONABLE.

OKAY, I'LL LEAVE YOUR TRAY OUTSIDE THE DOOR, THEN.

PLEASE TRY TO EAT AT LEAST A LITTLE.

FIGHT!
FIST!
FUNERAL!
CUP!
BRINGING YOU BEHIND-THE-MATCH COMMENTARY DAILY...
...YOUR FAVORITE ANCHORS...
JAYCE GIBSON!
AND KARL KLEIN!
FOR ITS 75TH SEASON...
...THE FFFC IS TAKING OVER THE WORLD'S TOP CHANNEL: LIVESPORT!

ALL THE INTERVIEWS, ALL THE NEWS...
Z
THE SCORES, ANALYSIS...
...FROM THE QUALIFYING ROUNDS TO THE FINAL.
CATCH THE BEST FIGHTS LIVE OR IN REPLAY!
AND TOMORROW, DON'T MISS...
FINISH YOUR PLATE, ADRIAN.
...IN THE KARL AND JAYCE REPORT...
FIST
...FOR HIS BIG RETURN TO FIGHTING, AN EXCLUSIVE INTERVIEW WITH...
TOMORRO
2:00 - 6:00
with KARL and JAYCE
BLIP!
OOOH! IT'S GONE...
YOUR MOTHER'S RIGHT...
IT'S NOT HEALTHY TO WATCH TV WHILE EATING.
TV...
WOULD YOU CARE FOR DESSERT?
NO, THANK YOU. WE'RE GOING TO BED.

BY THE WAY, WE'LL NEED A RIDE TO THE TOURNAMENT TOMORROW.
OF COURSE. WHICH MATCH ARE YOU SEEING?
WE'LL BE FIGHTING.
FIGHTING?
UM...
HOW SO?
ME AND MY MOM ARE IN THE TOURNAMENT.
TOGETHER.
THANKS FOR DINNER; IT WAS DELICIOUS.
SAY GOOD NIGHT, ADRIAN.
GOOD NIGHT!
BUT THAT'S IMPOSSIBLE...
HOTEL
ANITRANS
ANITRANS
ParkView
HOTEL

HOW THE HELL DID THEY GET TO PAXTOWN?
DOES THIS MEAN SHE KNEW THE WAY?

I'VE GOT TO TALK TO HER.

HEY! OPEN UP!

I HAVE TO TALK TO–
SAVE YOUR BREATH FOR TV, ALDANA.
BOOM
BOOM

AS SOON AS MR. ZOTIS IS BACK FROM HIS HELICOPTER RIDE, WE'RE TAKING YOU AND YOUR BUDDY FOR AN INTERVIEW. MILO WOULDN'T MISS THAT FOR ANYTHING.
...

MR. ZOTIS, WE'VE ARRIVED!

HOW'S THAT MEAT COMING ALONG?
MILO! IGNORING THE DRESS CODE YET AGAIN, I SEE!
MY DEAR ENRICO, I LOVE TRADITION, BUT WITHIN REASON!
WE WERE JUST TALKING ABOUT YOU!
HMM?
YES, WONDERING WHAT YOU HAVE UP YOUR SLEEVE THIS YEAR.
HAVE A BEER...
CONGRATS ON TOMIE GOING PLATINUM, BY THE WAY!
HAVEN'T YOU GOT ANYTHING BETTER THAN THIS DISHWATER?
THOSE ARE THE RULES OF THE BARBECUE, MILO... MUST I REMIND YOU EVERY TIME?
BEER AND HOT DOGS TAKE ON A SPECIAL FLAVOR ONCE YOU'VE MADE IT TO THE TOP!

AND THEN HE SAYS...

"THAT NEW DOPE HAS TAKEN OVER THE MARKET- WE CAN'T HELP IT!"

SO I SAID TO HIM, "ARE YOU KIDDING ME?"

"SOME PUNK IS SCREWING WITH OUR LIVELIHOODS AND 'YOU CAN'T HELP IT'?"

PFFF...

TWO BULLETS TO THE HEAD LATER, HE FINALLY GOT THE POINT!

THERE'RE STILL SOME RIBS AND HOT DOGS OVER HERE!

SO WHAT'S THIS NEW DRUG?

IT'S KIND OF LIKE SECTOR, BUT-

WRONG! IT *IS* SECTOR!

THOSE CLEVER LITTLE DICKWEEDS ARE PUSHING OUR OWN STUFF...

EXACTLY, IT'S GOOD OL' SECTOR. SOME OF MY GIRLS USE IT.
WHAT? EVEN YOUR SUPERSTAR?
NAH...TOMIE DOESN'T NEED THAT TO HIT ROCK BOTTOM!
FRIENDS, I HAVE SOME BIG NEWS FOR YOU...
I'VE GOT A HUNCH HE'S ABOUT TO TALK ABOUT DEAR OLD ALDANA.
SO DID YOU FIND HIM SWIMMING IN ALL THAT DAMN MONEY HE OWES US?
WHO WANTS A BURGER?

WITH HALF OF PAXTOWN AFTER HIM, I DON'T KNOW HOW HE MANAGED TO STAY ALIVE...
I'M SORRY TO SAY IT, GUYS, BUT WE'RE GONNA HAVE TO FORGET ABOUT THE MONEY.
FORGET?
FOR *TWO YEARS* OUR ACCOUNTANTS HAVE BEEN CLAMORING FOR IT!
HA!
WHAT I'M ABOUT TO OFFER YOU IS FAR MORE EXCITING THAN A FEW GRAND...
WE'RE ALL EARS.
RETURNING THE DISGRACED STAR TO THE FFFC...
...AND HIS DEATH ON LIVE TV, SEEN BY MILLIONS IN THE FINAL FIGHT!

THE CHAMPION'S FACE IS A STUDY IN CONCENTRATION...
SO FUN
15:00
THIS IS HIS MOMENT TO TAKE THE LEAD.
HOLD ON...
WE INTERRUPT THIS PROGRAM FOR A SPECIAL BULLETIN...
karl and jayce
breaking news
THANKS, JOHN-PAUL.
ON LIVESPORT, BREAKING NEWS CAN'T WAIT. AND HAVE WE GOT SOME EXCITING STUFF!

AFTER SEVERAL YEARS IN EXILE FOLLOWING HIS SHOCKING BEHAVIOR...
...THE MAN WHOSE NAME HAS LIVED ON IN INFAMY...
Richard Aldana
Cristo Canyon
RICHARD "NO SHAME" ALDANA!
HE WAS KICKED OUT OF THE LEAGUE...
...FOR ASSAULTING HIS PARTNER, DUKE DIAMONDS...
...AND EVEN WORSE, FOR SPITTING ON THE BELT BEFORE THE FINAL FIGHT.
MOM! RICHARD'S ON TV!
CHAMPION OF THE YEAR

...TRULY REVOLTING, KARL.
HE'S ABOUT TO SPEAK.
BUT... BESIDE HIM... THAT'S...
IT IS WITH GREAT JOY THAT I ANNOUNCE MY RETURN TO THE FFFC.
THE HEADS OF THE LEAGUE HAVE FOUND IT IN THEIR HEARTS TO PARDON MY DEPLORABLE ACTIONS...
WITH THEIR AGREEMENT AND IN ACCORDANCE WITH TOURNAMENT RULES, I WILL BE TEAMING UP WITH MR. CANYON, THE FIGHTER BY MY SIDE TODAY.
RICHARD!
MR. ALDANA? JAYCE, FOR LIVESPORT.
REGARDING YOUR PAST MISDEEDS... DO YOU HAVE ANY REGRETS?

CERTAINLY! I WANT TO APOLOGIZE TO THE LEAGUE, AND THE FANS.

AREN'T YOU AFRAID OF FACING YOUR FORMER OPPONENTS?

I TRUST IN THEIR SENSE OF HONOR, AND I PROMISE TO PROVE MY WORTH IN THE RING.

HEH HEH! YOU COULD ALMOST BUY IT!
GOOD OL' RICHARD!

CLOSE-UP ON HIS FACE!

BERTHA PEYTON FOR BB5 TV.
SO WHAT CAUSED THAT VIOLENT ALTERCATION WITH YOUR EX-PARTNER...

...DUKE DIAMONDS?

NO COMMENT.
ALDANA!
HOW DARE YOU SHOW YOUR FACE AROUND HERE!
YOU SON OF A BITCH!
BANUS!
APOLOGIZE AS MUCH AS YOU WANT, I'LL STILL GONNA RIP YOU APART IN THE RING! AND THIS TIME, YOU CAN'T RUN AWAY...
BANUS
I'LL BE WAITING—FOR YOU *AND* YOUR WIMPY BALLERINA!

THERE'S NO PLACE FOR YOU IN THE FFFC, AND I'M GONNA SEE THAT THE WHOLE WORLD KNOWS IT.
BANUS
DULY NOTED, BANUS. THANKS.
I HOPE YOU MANAGED TO WIN A FEW TITLES IN MY ABSENCE.
SEE, MOM? IT'S CRISTO!

SCUMBAG! I'LL TEACH YOU AND YOUR CLOWN A THING OR TWO IN THE FINAL!
CAMERA 2: CLOSE-UP ON CANYON.
DZZz
MR. CANYON!
WHERE ARE YOU FROM?
WHY ALDANA?
...

MR. CANYON...
ANY WORDS
FOR ZOTIS
LIVESPORT?

MR. CANYON...?

THWA!
THWA!

THWA! THWA!
STRIKE WITH YOUR FISTS AND SUMMON WITH YOUR MIND.
AT THE SAME TIME?
YES, AT THE SAME TIME.
BUT HOW?
COME ON, FOCUS...
BOC! BOC!

QUALIFYING
ROUND 1
OKAY, LET'S START..."QUALIFIERS"... NO..."WHO WILL MAKE THE FINAL ROUND?"
RING 3
GROUP B
RING 12
NO...
HMM...I'LL JUST PUT "TITLE" FOR NOW.
I'LL FIND SOMETHING CATCHIER LATER ON.
TEAM KARL & JAMES, QUALIFIED FOR THE SECOND ROUND...
...BY K.O.
YEAH, BUT WE CAN'T FIND THEIR OPPONENTS.
WHEE...
THEY'RE MOVING TO THIS RING.
CLAP.
THE LEAGUE OKAYED IT?
MEDIC!
HMM...
SO... "AS WITH EVERY YEAR..."
"...A SPARSE CROWD OF CONNOISSEURS HAS GATHERED IN THE WESTERN WING OF ZOTIS STADIUM FOR..."
NO, THAT'S TERRIBLE...

"HOW SAD TO SEE THE QUALIFYING ROUNDS DRAW SUCH LIMITED INTEREST..."
"...THE CROWDS TURNING OUT ONLY FOR THE STARS."
"NAMES LIKE BANUS, TSUNA MIKE, OR ANOTHER SASHA YOUNG..."
"IT'S THE REAL FANS OF THE SPORT WHO ARE HERE..."
"...SEEKING OUT DIAMONDS IN THE ROUGH."
"THEY EXCHANGE KNOWING GLANCES..."
ZZZ...
"AWARE THAT..."
"THE BEST SURPRISES EMERGE HERE."
"FOR IT IS HERE THAT YOURS TRULY SAW THE BREAKOUT DEBUTS OF CORDOBA, JESSIE JAW..."
"...AND, OF COURSE..."
the breakout debuts
RDOBA, JESSIE JAW
urse RICHARD ALD_

HEY THERE, MARIANNE!
OH, HI!
DID YOU GET BACK ALL RIGHT LAST TIME?
SO YOU'RE HERE TO WATCH THE QUALIFIERS?
ACTUALLY, WE'RE HERE TO FIGHT. OUR MATCH IS IN AN HOUR.
OH, RIGHT!
I IMAGINE YOU HAVE A NICE VIEW UP THERE.
OH YES, YOU BET! HEE HEE!
ENJOY THE SHOW, THEN.
THANKS. YOU TOO!
TAP
TAP
TAP
TAP
TAP

THIS ISN'T A DAMN PLAYGROUND. HE'LL NEED AT LEAST SOME PADS. IF YOU DON'T HAVE ANY, SEE THE STAFF ABOUT IT.

WHY DO I HAVE TO WEAR THIS?

THERE'S MY HANDSOME LITTLE FIGHTER!

IT'S THE RULES HERE... THAT'S THE WAY IT IS.
I'M TOO HOT.
NOW, REMEMBER...

IF I PUT MY HAND IN THE RING...

...WHAT DO YOU DO?

SLAP!
STAFF

HEY, WE'RE UP IN TEN MINUTES...
CAN I GO FIRST?
SURE YOU CAN, ADRIAN.
P(34/35/36)
RING

CRAP...
BiP.
BiP.
AND BIG FAT JOE CEDES THE POINT TO HIS DISTRICT...
BiP.
THE RODEO V6 SPUN OFF THE TRACK...
BiP.
THE WILDCATS SCORE!!!
KEEP YOUR SKIN SOFT WITH-
NOT ONE DAMN CHANNEL SHOWING THE FIGHTS.
AT LEAST LET ME TALK TO H!
SHUT UP!
MILO SAID YOU NEED TO REST.
CRACK
THAT'S RIGHT, BREAK STUFF...

DAMN IT!

!!!
HUH?
IS THIS A JOKE?!
NO.

A MOM AND KID?
THEY'RE ALLOWED TO FIGHT; THEY GOT A WAIVER.
THE LEAGUE SIGNED OFF ON IT.
LISTEN, I'M NOT HITTING A KID...
ESPECIALLY IN FRONT OF HIS MOM.

YOU'RE FREE TO FORFEIT, IF IT BOTHERS YOU SO MUCH.
THIS IS INSANE—THE LEAGUE WILL BE HEARING FROM ME!

A CHICK...
...AND A DWARF?
MARIANNE?
OKAY, GENTLEMEN... LADY...
YOUR ATTENTION, PLEASE.
THIS IS A TAG-TEAM MATCH. YOU SWITCH PARTNERS WITH A HAND SLAP. CLEAN FIGHTING ONLY: NO STRIKES BELOW THE BELT, AND NO FISH-HOOKING.
ANY RING-OUT, WALK-OFF, OR KNOCKOUT MEANS THE FIGHT IS OVER.
LADY, GENTLEMEN, TO YOUR CORNERS.
PFFF...WHAT A JOKE.
LOOK ON THE BRIGHT SIDE, GUYS.
WHAT'S THAT, COACH?
WITH THAT OPPOSITION, YOU'LL BE SAILING INTO THE SECOND ROUND.
THE MOM WON'T LET HER KID GO FIRST.
JUST CLEAR HER OUT WITHOUT GETTING TOO ROUGH.
AND THEN WE'RE ONTO THE SERIOUS STUFF.
THIS IS AN INSULT FROM THE LEAGUE!

GENTLEMEN, LADY: ONLY TWO FIGHTERS IN THE RING...
DING
DING
HAVE YOU MADE YOUR CHOICE?
...
SERIOUSLY?
WHAT THE HELL DO I DO?
SHE'S CRAZY...
?
THIS IS INSANE!
GO FOR IT, SWEETIE!
REMEMBER WHAT I TOLD YOU!

YEAH, BUT I'M TOO HOT, AND THE HELMET'S ITCHY!
...
TRY NOT TO THINK ABOUT IT!
BUT IT'S SUCH A PAIN!
WHAT SHOULD I DO?
BAH, JUST SHOVE HIM THROUGH THE THE ROPES...
BUT GENTLY!
DING!
LISTEN, KID, I'M NOT GONNA HURT YOU...COME CLOSER.
SPIRIT OF THE WIND...
WHAT?

THOOMBLAST!
KTRING!

SHLAM!
...
BOP!
CLAP CLAP
CONGRATULATIONS, SWEETIE!
EXCUSE ME, SIR?

HE'S OUT OF THE RING! DOES THAT MEAN I WON?
WHAT?
UH... YEAH!
RING OUT!

WOO HOO! IN ONE MOVE!
CLAP!
YOU SAW THAT?

CAN I GO FIRST NEXT TIME TOO?
YOU GOT IT!

Marion . S
Milo . Z .
MILO?
I'M BUSY, H!
YEAH, I KNOW, BUT YOU GOTTA COME SEE THIS!
IT'S THE KID AND HIS MOM.
WHAT?
WHO ARE THEY FIGHTING?
I'LL BE THERE IN 45 MINUTES!

TEAMS-
SELECT YOUR
FIGHTER!
DID
YOU SEE
THAT? ONE
STRIKE!
DON'T
TAKE ANY
CHANCES!
READY TO
TRY THE WASP
MOVE?
YEAH!
I
WON'T.
FIGHT!
GO
ADRIAN!
THOMP

SWERVE!
!!!
TBAM!
GET OVER HERE!
SWERVE!
SWERVE!
STING!

PAK!
ARGH!
I FORGOT THE
SUMM–
WHACK

POW!
THUNK!
ADRIAN!
TAG ME IN!
TEN!
NINE!

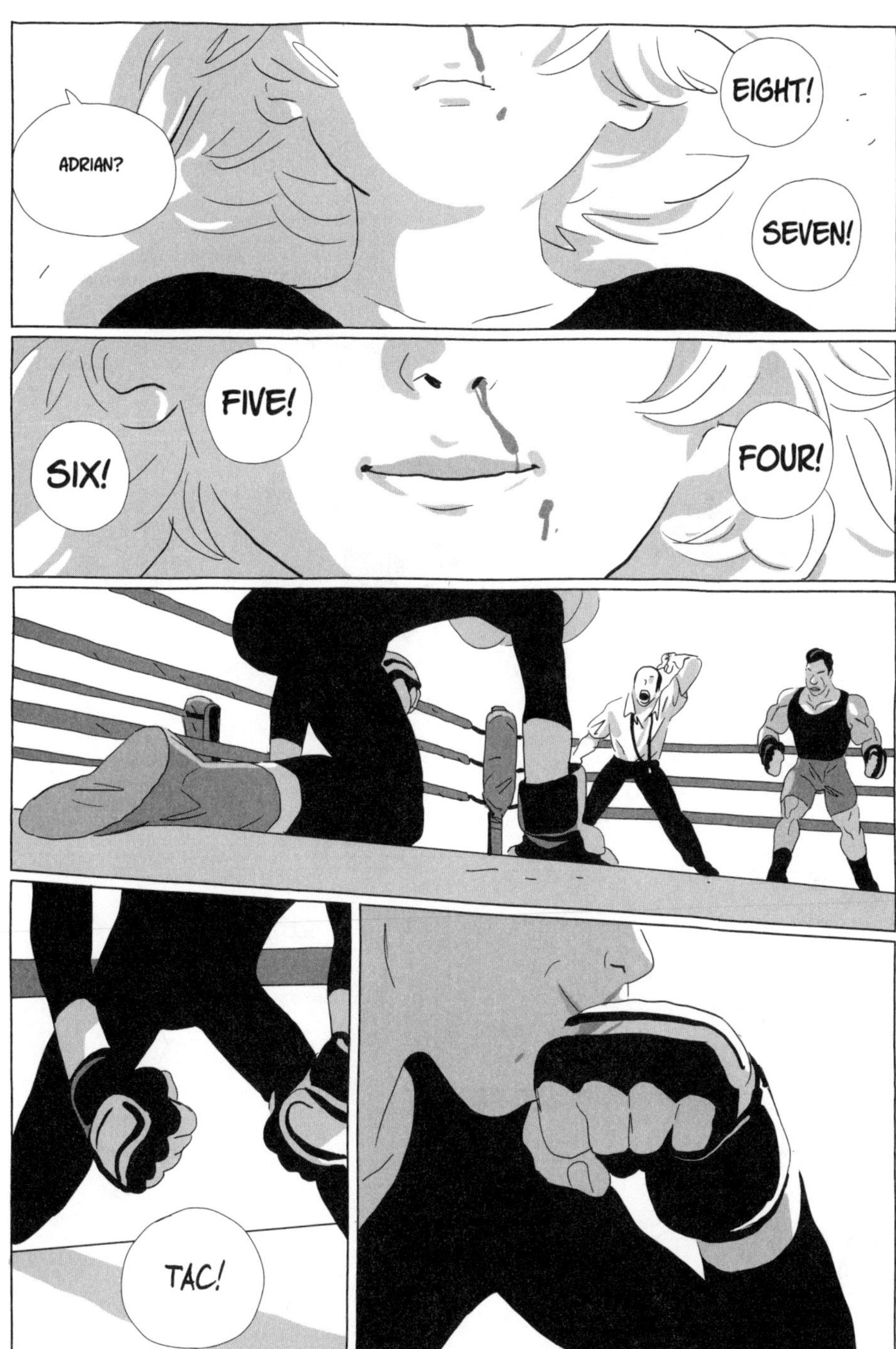
ADRIAN?
EIGHT!
SEVEN!
SIX!
FIVE!
FOUR!
TAC!

I'VE GOT THIS, MOM!
DON'T WORRY; I'LL LEAVE YOU THE OTHER GUY.
?
RESUME!

HOW THE HELL IS THIS BRAT STILL STANDING?
I DIDN'T HIT FULL STRENGTH, BUT STILL...
I WON'T BE MADE A FOOL OF BY SOME TWERP!
HE'S NOT GETTING UP FROM THIS ONE!
YAAAA!
STOMP!

YOU UNDERSTAND, ADRIAN?
YOU'LL HAVE TO USE A LOT OF MAGIC...
...IN BOTH ATTACK AND DEFENSE.
YOUR OPPONENTS WILL BE BIGGER AND TOUGHER. YOU'LL NEED TO SUPRISE THEM WITH THE MAGIC OF THE ELEMENTS.
OKAY, LET'S TRY A SIMPLE DEFENSE!
SPIRIT OF THE WIND, FROM BEYOND THE MOUNTAINS...

...PROTECT ME!!!

TORRENT
UNLEASH!
WOOOOO-SHH!

WHAT THE...
WILL YOU TEACH ME THE SCHOOL-OF-HEAVENS SUMMONING?
YES, BUT YOU HAVE TO MASTER THIS ONE FIRST.
IT'S THE FOUNDATION FOR REACHING THE HIGHER LEVEL.
FLOOOSHH!

SPLAT!
?!!
WHAT'S THIS RUCKUS AROUND RING 5?

DID A PIPE BURST, OR WHAT?
HOLY COW!
I DID THE TORRENT ATTACK!
I'M SO PROUD OF YOU, SWEETIE!
MR. REFEREE?
HUH? UM...
RIGHT!

OUT!

I WON!

HE THREW HIM FROM THE RING?
I SWEAR-I SAW IT WITH MY OWN EYES!
BUT ...*HOW?*
WHAT-?

ADRIAN VELBA WINS!

YAAAAH!

THANKS, MOM! YOUR MOVES ARE AWESOME!

WE'RE GONNA WIN!

HA!

GOOD GOD! THAT LITTLE RUNT COULD DAMN WELL WIN THE FFFC!
CALL FIONA!
BUT, MORE IMPORTANT...

...GET ME RICHARD!
HOTEL
I WAS GOOD ENOUGH FOR THE FFFC TOO, YOU KNOW?
SURE YOU WERE.
HOTEL

I'M THINKING JESSIE JAW OR BANUS THIS YEAR.
BANUS? YOU KIDDING? HE'LL FALL FLAT ON HIS FACE, LIKE ALWAYS...
IT WASN'T 'CAUSE YOU FIGHT LIKE A GIRL?
I HAD HIM AS A SPARRING PARTNER, ACTUALLY...
SCREW YOU!
HE MESSED UP MY KNEE AND I COULDN'T GO PRO.
HANG ON, I GOT A MESSAGE FROM H.
BEEP!
WHAT'D HE SAY?
WE GOTTA BRING PRINCESS ALDANA TO THE STADIUM.
WELL, IT'S ABOUT TIME. I WAS STARTING TO GET CRAMPS.
IN YOUR KNEE?
WOULD YOU JUST QUIT IT?
KNOCK!
HEY, ALD-
?
SLAM!!!

WHAT?
N...
HEY, TUBBY! ENOUGH WITH THE BABY-SITTING!
GNNN...
I'VE GOT SOMETHING TO SAY TO MILO!
NOW GIVE ME YOUR CAR KEYS!
AAARGH...
MY NOSE!
OR I'LL-
OKAY, OKAY.
WHAT'S THAT?
OKAY.
W...WE WERE ABOUT TO TAKE YOU...MILO WANTS YOU AT THE STADIUM...
OH.
YEAH.
OKAY.
DAMN IT.
HEY, MOVE IT!
I CAN'T SEE!
QUIT SHOVING!

HOLY CRAP!
DID YOU SEE THAT?
WHA...
WHAT...
THIS KID'S UNBELIEVABLE.
H...HOW'D HE DO THAT?
HUFF...
HUFF...
GO ADRIAN!
BUT LET ME KNOW IF YOU'RE TIRED.
THE GREATEST BOXERS IN THE COUNTRY...
...LAID LOW BY A BOY AND HIS MOTHER.
I THINK I'VE GOT THE START OF MY NEXT ARTICLE.
LISTEN, KID, I–
MOVE IT!
HUH?

SWITCH OVER; YOU'RE MAKING A FOOL OF YOURSELF.
BESIDES...
FOWLER.
I'VE ALWAYS LOVED PLAYING WITH KIDDIES.

ADRIAN—
TAG ME IN.
WAIT.
ADRIAN!
BUT, MOM...
IT'S OKAY, I CAN BEAT HIM!
WHAT DID I TELL YOU?
WHEN I EXTEND MY HAND, YOU TAP IT.
GOT THAT?
OTHERWISE, WE'RE GOING HOME!
SO LITTLE CHICKY'S GONE BACK TO ITS NEST?
WHAT A SHAME!
GUESS I'LL JUST HAVE TO SETTLE FOR MAMA BIRD.

HEH HEH HEH...
COME TO DADDY!

AAARGH...
KRAAK
HOLY...
WOO HOOO...
DID THAT JUST HAPPEN?!
DAMN!
SHE BLEW UP THE STANDS!
WAIT, RICHARD... *THAT'S* THE GIRL YOU SEDUCED AND SCREWED?
HA HA HA!!!
YOU'RE IN FOR SOME SERIOUS HELL, BUDDY.

AND NOW, DIRECT FROM LIVESPORT STUDIOS...
karl and jayce live report
...YOUR WEEKLY *LIVE REPORT* WITH EVERYONE'S FAVORITE DUO...
KAAAAARL AND JAYYYYCE!!!
YEEEAH
GOOD EVENING!
CLAP
CLAP!
WOOO!
THANKS FOR JOINING US FOR THIS EXTRA-SPECIAL *LIVE REPORT* ON THE FFFC!
CLAP
CLAP
YOU GUYS ARE ON FIRE TONIGHT!
CLAP!
AS YOU ALL KNOW, THE QUALIFYING ROUNDS ENDED FRIDAY!
AND, BELIEVE ME, THIS IS HUGE NEWS!
ALMOST AS HUGE AS YOUR BEHIND, KARL!
HA HA HA
IN FACT, A MOST UNEXPECTED PAIR BURST ONTO THE SCENE—AS OUR VIEWERS WILL SOON FIND OUT!

STEVE, YOU ALMOST DONE WITH MAKEUP?
UM...NO. THERE'S AN ISSUE.
AND HOW 'BOUT THE NEWS, JAYCE!
WE NEED THEM READY TO ROLL IN TWENTY MINUTES. STUDIO 3.
WELL, I'LL TRY.
THE GOVERNMENT'S LATEST STATEMENT ON DOPING SURE MADE AN IMPACT!
YEAH, KARL, YOU'D BETTER HIDE THOSE HIPPO-DERIVED ANITRANS!
HA HA HA
WHAT'S THE DAMN PROBLEM?
IT'S, UH, THE MOM. SHE...
NO! ABSOLUTELY OUT OF THE QUESTION!
HOW DO I PUT IT?
THERE'S A DISAGREEMENT WITH PUBLICITY...
PLEASE, MARIANNE. MR. ZOTIS HIMSELF CHOSE IT.
IT'S YOUR OFFICIAL FIGHTING OUTFIT!
WHAT, THIS? FOR FIGHTING?
YOU'VE GOT TO BE KIDDING!

WHO FIGHTS IN A GETUP LIKE THIS?

I'M PRACTICALLY NAKED! EVEN AT FRANCIS'S THE GIRLS WORE MORE THAN THIS!

UM...

YES, BUT... MILO WON'T-

SCREW MILO!

SHE'S RIGHT! IT'S RIDICULOUS!

TOMIE! WE'RE KIND OF BUSY HERE...
WOULD YOU MIND LEAVING US FOR A BIT?
GET OUT, FIONA!
HEY! CAN I WEAR THIS?
...
SHALL WE GO BACKSTAGE FOR THE TOUCH-UPS?
IT'S JUST SOME OLD T-SHIRT OF MINE. DO WHATEVER YOU WANT–I DON'T CARE!

SLAM!

HEY, WAIT!

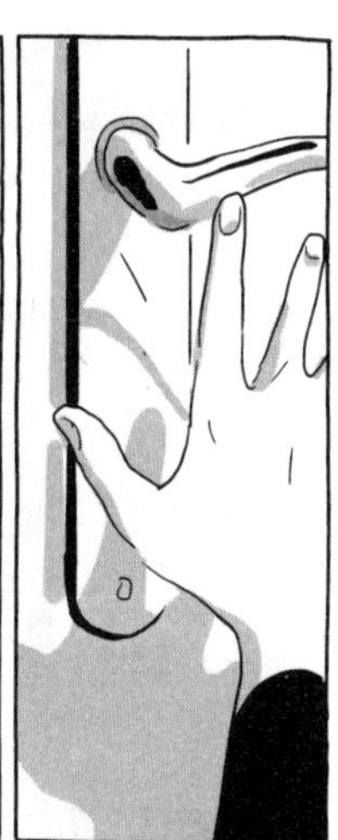

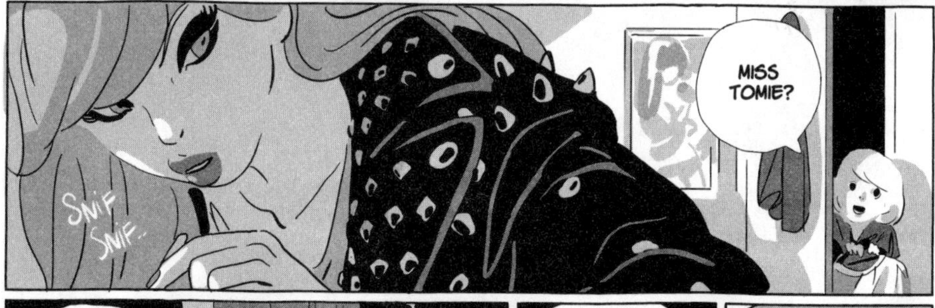
SNIF SNIF...
MISS TOMIE?

WHAT NOW?

UM...CAN I CUT OFF THE SLEEVES?

I SAID I DON'T CARE!

WELL, ALDANA'S RETURN HAS SENT HALF THE LEAGUE ON THE WARPATH!
HARDLY SURPRISING, OF COURSE, CONSIDERING ALL THE INFLAMMATORY STUFF HE SAID...
HA HA!
AFTER SIX MONTHS OF INTENSE TRAINING AT AN UNDERWATER FACILITY, JESSIE JAW'S BACK IN TOP FORM...
AND FOR THOSE OF YOU WHO MISSED *EATING TOWER*, THE REALITY SHOW OF THE SUMMER...
...I CAN TELL YOU OUR FRIEND TYPHOON'S GUNNING FOR THE TOP SPOT!
YOU'RE ON IN TEN SECONDS!
WELL, AREN'T YOU THE SQUEALING FANGIRL, JAYCE.
HA HA HA

CLAP
OH, BEHAVE, KARL!
CLAP
CLAP
AND NOW IT'S TIME TO WELCOME THE TEAM THAT COULD OUTSHINE ALL OF THEM!
TAP TAP
GO!
MARIANNE AND ADRIAN...
VELLLLBA!
UH...
CLAP
WELCOME TO *LIVE REPORT*. HAVE A SEAT!
UM...

HELLO!

WOOOOOOOOOOOOOO
AWWW!

ADOOORABLE! AND HOW OLD IS THE LITTLE PRINCE?
TWELVE AND A HALF!
WOW!

DEAR VIEWERS...
IF YOU'RE JUST JOINING US, THIS IS, OF COURSE, THE SPECIAL FFFC EDITION OF *LIVE REPORT*, AND THESE TWO REMARKABLE GUESTS ARE THE BIG WINNERS OF THE QUALIFYING ROUNDS.

ADRIAN! PLEASE TELL OUR VIEWERS JUST HOW YOU MANAGED TO KNOCK OUT SUCH FEARSOME FIGHTERS!

IT WAS EASY, I JUST DID WHAT MY MOM SAID.
OOOOOOOOOOOOOOH
THIS IS GOLDEN!
HE'S GOT THEM EATING OUT OF HIS HAND.
LOVELY! AND WHAT ABOUT YOU, MARIANNE? ARE YOU AFFILIATED WITH A CLUB?
UM, NO... I'M A BAKER.
A BAKER? IS THAT SO?
TEE HEE!
POUNDING DOUGH MUST MAKE FOR GOOD TRAINING!
HA HA HA HA
WHOA THERE, KARL!
BUT TELL US, MARIANNE... WHY DID YOU WANT TO BE IN THE TOURNAMENT?
WERE YOU THAT BORED WITH WORKING THE OVEN?
WELL...
I'VE HEARD IT HAD SOMETHING TO DO WITH...
...RICHARD ALDANA.

PFFF!
ANOTHER ONE OF MILO'S BRIGHT IDEAS!
IS IT TRUE? DO YOU HAVE TIES WITH ALDANA?
I DON'T KNOW WHERE YOU HEARD THAT...
...BUT I HAVE NOTHING TO DO WITH THAT MAN.
I KNOW ABOUT HIS REPUTATION, LIKE EVERYONE ELSE...
BUT THAT'S IT!

Super
No.1 Stars!
OMG!
Truly Yours
1,50 ₫
Best News, unbeatable Price
EACH WEEK
TOMIE KATANA
RICHARD ALDANA
They were in heaven, Now they're in HELL
ANITRANS
Your favorite stars tell us how we can benefit too
FASHION
ELLINGTOWN STYLE
75
Velba Aldana
What really happened? And what about Tomie??
Tomie
Responds to the return of
All the dirt on the romance between
TOMIE & RICHARD
INVESTIGATION
JUST PERFECT!
MARIANNE AND ADRIAN
The cutest team in the FFFC
tomie Katana
HOW WILL SHE REACT?
ALDANA AND MARIANNE
Was It Just Sex...Or Real Love?
What's driving so many addicts to suicide?

WE COULDN'T HAVE HOPED FOR BETTER! THE PRESS IS ALL OVER IT!

NICE WORK, FIONA.

THANK YOU, MR. ZOTIS.

IS EVERYTHING READY FOR THE PARTY TONIGHT?

EVERY-ONE WHO'S ANYONE WILL BE THERE.

GOOD.

OBVIOUSLY, I'LL WANT TOMIE THERE–SHE CAN SING HER NEW SINGLE. SO SHE BETTER NOT PULL ONE OF HER "I'M SO SICK" ROUTINES.

THE VICTOR IS PROUD TO WELCOME THE GREATEST BOXERS OF THE FFFC!
JESSIE JAW, YOU'RE NUMBER ONE IN THE RING AND ON THE DANCE FLOOR– WHAT'S YOUR SECRET?
SHE'S NUMBER ONE, NOT ME!
WE WISH THEM GOOD LUCK FOR THE FINAL ROUNDS!
V.I.P.
?
!
HE ACTUALLY HAD THE GALL TO COME...

LOSE THE CAMERA! LIVESPORT'S GOT THE EXCLUSIVE RIGHTS.

SMILE! THERE ARE PLENTY OF GUYS HERE WHO'LL BE HAPPY TO SEE YOU.

CLAP!

SO, WHAT? YOU GONNA BABYSIT ME ALL NIGHT?

HE'S MINE!

THE BASTARD!

YUP, JUST LIKE OLD TIMES!
NOW, DON'T GET SMASHED, ALDANA. YOU'RE ALREADY A SORRY SIGHT IN THE RING.
DOM!
DOM!
YOU'RE A REAL COMEDIAN, YOU KNOW THAT?
DON'T MESS AROUND— WE'LL BE WATCHING.
DOM!
DOM!
MARIANNE!
COME DOWN!
DOM!
DOM!

FIONA, THINK YOU COULD WATCH ADRIAN FOR A FEW MINUTES?
OF COURSE.
STAY WITH FIONA, OKAY?
YUP!
YOU LIKE VIDEO GAMES, ADRIAN?
I DUNNO.
WHAT'S A VIDEO?
LET'S GO; I'LL SHOW YOU.
OKAY.
DOM!
DOM!
DOM!
DOM!
DOM!
DOM!
DOM
DOM!
DOM!
DOM!
DOM!

YOU'VE GOT NO BUSINESS HERE!
YOU HAVE NO GODDAMN CLUE WHAT'S GOING ON...
...AND YOU'RE DRAGGING ADRIAN INTO IT, TOO!
YOU'RE BOTH GOING BACK TO THE VALLEY–
NOW!
DON'T YOU GET IT?
YOU'RE IN DANGER HERE!

I WAS ALREADY UP THE CREEK WITHOUT A PADDLE—I DIDN'T NEED YOU COMING IN AND MAKING THINGS EVEN WORSE!
SO YOU'RE GONNA LISTEN UP AND GET THE HELL OUT OF PAXTOWN...
NO, YOU LISTEN!
RUNNING OFF IS *YOUR* SPECIALTY.
AND I KNOW WHAT TO MAKE OF YOUR PROMISES!
DON'T YOU WORRY ABOUT ADRIAN AND ME— WE MANAGE JUST FINE WITHOUT YOU!
GREAT! SO WHY COME HERE AND BUST MY BALLS?
WHAT DO YOU GET OUT OF IT?!
ALDANA, IF I MEET YOU IN THAT RING, I SWEAR I'LL—

YEAH, THANKS! HAVE A GOOD NIGHT.

HONESTLY, YOU SUCK, ALDANA. YOU'RE GONNA GET SHREDDED.

YEAH, YEAH, BEAT IT.

WHAT YOU SAID TO ADRIAN...

I HOPE YOU DIDN'T MEAN IT.

DOES THIS MAP LOOK FAMILIAR?

WHAT THE...

WHERE DID YOU FIND THAT?

I'M THE ONE ASKING QUESTIONS HERE.

GIVE IT BACK!

DOM!
PRIVATE
DOM! DOM!
DOM!

DOM! DOM!

LAME-ASS PARTY!

CRUNCH!

AH, TOMIE!
DO ME A FAVOR, WOULD YOU?
HMM?
KEEP AN EYE ON ADRIAN...
...WHILE I DEAL WITH THE REPORTERS.
STAY WITH TOMIE, SWEETIE.
THANKS, DARLING!
FIONA, WAIT...
CLACK!
...

THIS IS MY PIECE. I HAD IT IN THE VALLEY– IT'S HOW I CAME ALL THIS WAY.
AND THAT'S YOUR PIECE– I RECOVERED IT IN THE NILLIPOLIS COURTROOM.
VALLEY OF KINGS
FOREST
MIDDLE PASSAGE
SOUTHERN VOLCANOES
EXIT FROM THE MINE
YOU'RE THE ONE WHO HAD THE OTHER HALF?
YES.
ADRIAN'S FATHER DREW THE MAP. I SUCCEEDED IN KEEPING HALF OF IT BEFORE HE LEFT.
VALLEY OF KINGS
FOREST
CACTI DESERT
RIDGE TO THE VALLEY
DAMN...

SO ADRIAN'S FATHER ISN'T FROM THE VALLEY OF KINGS?
SEEMS LIKE YOU'VE GOT A SOFT SPOT FOR FOREIGNERS...
HOW DID YOU GET THIS MAP, RICHARD?
YOU WANT TO KNOW IF I STOLE IT FROM ADRIAN'S FATHER?
FIRST, I DIDN'T STEAL IT– I WON IT IN AN UNDERGROUND BOXING FIGHT.
SECOND, IT WASN'T ADRIAN'S DAD.
...UNLESS I'M REALLY MISTAKEN ABOUT YOUR TASTE IN MEN.

SELECT YOUR PLAYER.
CRACK-JACK
CRYSTAL
UM... WHAT'S THAT?
IT LOOKS LIKE TV!
WAIT, YOU'VE NEVER SEEN A VIDEO GAME?
WOW, YOU GUYS ARE REALLY FROM THE BOONDOCKS!
NO!
DO YOU AT LEAST KNOW HOW TO USE A TOILET?
HUH?
NEVER MIND. PRESS THE START BUTTON AND GRAB THE JOYSTICK.
HERE?
YEAH.

THIS IS FOR PUNCHING.
THAT'S TO KICK.
K.O.!
WHAT? WE LOST ALREADY?
TIP TICK
TICK
HERE, LET'S USE AN EASIER FIGHTER...
TICK
HOW ABOUT THE GUY WITH THE GREEN ARMOR?
TIP TAP
TICK
TIP TIP
NO, HE'S STUPID!
HEY...IS THAT RICHARD?
YEAH; THIS GAME'S KINDA OLD. YOU CAN CHOOSE HIM IF YOU WANT.
NO!
THE ONE NEXT TO HIM, WITH HORNS!

NOW GET READY! YOU'LL BE FIGHTING ON THE RIGHT.
GOT IT?
YES!

DAMN...

SEEING ALDANA STRUTTING AROUND LIKE A PEACOCK MAKES ME WANT TO...

WELL, IF IT ISN'T MRS. ALDANA, THE POP PRINCESS!

HEY, BEAUTIFUL!
YOU HAPPY ABOUT GETTING YOUR RICHARD BACK?

AND PLAYIN' NANNY TO HIS KID, TOO! HOW SWEET.

YOU'RE ONE OBEDIENT GIRL, AREN'T YOU?

ALWAYS DOING WHAT YOU'RE TOLD: SING, SMILE, EAT...

MARRY THIS GUY!

WEAR THAT BIKINI!

TAKE IT OFF!

RIGHT, TOMIE?

WHATCHA STARIN' AT?

HEY, RUNT! I ASKED YOU A QUESTION!

LEAVE HIM ALONE, BANUS.
MOVE IT.

HEY, I'M TALKING TO YOU!

TIME'S UP!
...
SO WHAT HAPPENED TO YOUR MAGICAL POWERS?
THEY DON'T WORK WHEN MOMMY'S NOT AROUND?
SHE'S COMING BACK!
OH YEAH?
YOU SEE THAT SCAR ALL OVER MY FACE?
I GOT IT THE FIRST TIME I WENT INTO THE RING, WHEN A GUY STOMPED ON MY HEAD.
I WAS ABOUT THE SAME AGE AS YOU...

ADRIAN! WAIT!
BLAM
HEH HEH!
SO THAT'S THE PRODIGY THEY'RE SAYING WILL UPEND THE LEAGUE?
HA HA!
HEE HEE!
YOU'RE AN ASSHOLE, BANUS!
HA!

DOM!
DOM!
DOM!
DOM!
DOM!
DOM!
DOM!
AW, HE'S SO CUTE!
DOM!
DOM!
DOM!
WATCH IT!
DOM!
DOM!
DOM!
WOOO!
OH...
CRAP...
DOM!
DOM!
DAMN!
DOM!
WHAT THE...
HA
HA!
MY GOD, WATCH WHERE YOU'RE GOING!!
DOM!
DOM!

DOM!
DOM!
DOM!
THAT WAS A $400 BOTTLE!!!
DOM!
DOM!
DOM!
GET BACK HERE!
DOM!
PRIVATE
TOMIE...
DOM!
DOM!
DOM!
DOM!

...
MMM...
CLANG!
!!!
CLICK
CLICK
HEY...
PSST...
HEY...
KID...

FIX...
COME ON...GNN...KID... JUST A FEW BUCKS...
I NEED MY FIX...
EVEN IF YOU THINK ADRIAN'S HAPPY HERE, YOU TWO NEED TO RETURN TO THE VALLEY... TRUST ME.
BAM! BAM!
HEY, YOU TWO! DO YOU MIND?!
BAM!
GET A ROOM! SOME OF US ACTUALLY HAVE TO TAKE A DUMP!

ALL RIGHT, ALL RIGHT!
TWO MINUTES!
HOW LONG HAVE WE BEEN HERE?
I LEFT ADRIAN UPSTAIRS.
I HOPE FIONA KEPT HER EYES ON HIM.

DOM!
WATCH IT!
DOM!
DOM!
SORRY!
WHOA!
IT'S TOMIE!
TOMIE?!
I LOVED "KISS ME MAYBE"!
DID A BLOND KID COME THROUGH HERE?
TOMIE?! WHERE ARE YOUR BODYGAURDS?
DOM!
DOM!

MISS KATANA?
DOM!
YOU'RE LOOKING FOR YOUNG ADRIAN?

YES! IS HE HERE?
DOM!
DOM!
I SAW HIM RUNNING ACROSS THE ROOM!

I'M PETER VERKAIK, BY THE WAY.
I GOT IT ON FILM!

GNNN... C'MON, KID... HAVE A HEART.
...
DON'T GO...
SSSH...
COME BACK...
ARE YOU LOST?

ADRIAN!
!

OH!
MISS TOMIE!

EVERYTHING GOOD? YOU FOUND HIM?
THAT'S MOM'S FRIEND!
THANK GOD HE SAW YOU! WHAT'D FIONA SAY? YOU'RE SUPPOSED TO STAY WITH ME.

MISS KATANA...
WE SHOULD RETURN TO THE PARTY. THE STREETS OF PAXTOWN AREN'T...

SHUT THE DOOR!
...SAFE.
IT'S FREEZING!

NO, WAIT! DON'T CLOSE THE-
SLAM!

YOU WERE AT THE PARTY, TOO?
HEY, OPEN UP!
BAM! BAM!
YOU SEE, ADRIAN... A PRO ALWAYS MANAGES TO...
ARE YOUR GLASSES BROKEN?
NO, NO... I'M OKAY.

DAMN IT!

UGH...
!!!
EXCUSE ME...

I'M NOT VIOLENT...
I JUST NEED MY FIX.

I'M CALLING FIONA. SHE'LL COME DOWN.
HE'S A TOX-COMPLETELY EATEN UP BY SECTOR...
STAY HERE, ADRIAN.
I'M WRITING AN ARTICLE ON IT.
IT HURTS...

THAT DRUG HAS A BASE OF ANITRANS HORMONES, BOOSTED WITH INSECT PROTEINS. IT INCREASES YOUR STRENGTH TENFOLD, MAKING YOU FEEL INVINCIBLE. IN RETURN, YOU GET A FRIED BRAIN, INSTANT ADDICTION, AND EXTREME VIOLENCE.
AAAAH...
YO, CHECK IT OUT!
?

I CAN'T BELIEVE IT!
GUYS!
GET OVER HERE!
YOUR CALL COULD NOT BE COMPLETED...

WELL I'LL BE DAMNED! TOMIE KATANA!

UGH...
BEAT IT, TOX!
CRAP.
SO TELL ME, BABE...
WHATCHA DOIN' OUT HERE?

BOM! BOM!
OPEN UP!

WHOA! IT'S REALLY YOU!
SERIOUSLY, YOU LOOK BETTER THAN ON TV!
SO HOW'D YA GET INTO SHOW BUSINESS?
I WANTED TO BE A SINGER...
...BUT THOSE BASTARDS NEVER GAVE ME A CHANCE.
HEY!
TOMIE, YOU THINK WE COULD START A BAND?
YOUR HONEST OPINION.
LOOK AT US!
WHY AREN'T YOU ANSWERING? IT'S RUDE NOT TO ANSWER!
YOU THINK YOU'RE SO HOT WITH YOUR BIG TITS?
IS THAT IT? YOU THINK YOU'RE HOT?

GIMME THAT!
YOU DON'T NEED IT!

YOU KNOW WHAT? MAYBE WE CAN'T BREAK INTO SHOWBIZ, BUT WE CAN AT LEAST HAVE SOME FUN WITH A STAR.
CLAP!
HOW'S THAT SOUND?

FLASH!
?

LEAVE HER ALONE! CAN'T YOU SEE THERE'S A KID HERE?
FLASH!
YOU OUGHT TO BE ASH-

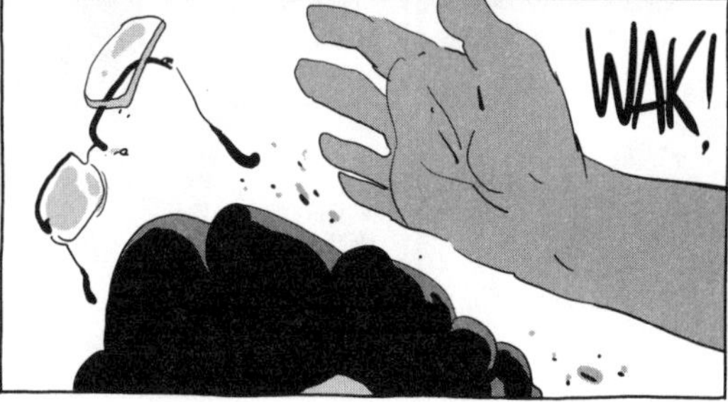
WAK!

GODDAMN FOUR-EYES!!!

WHO THE HELL DO YOU THINK YOU ARE?

AAARGH...

TAKIN' PICTURES OF US...

HOW ABOUT OUR RIGHT TO PRIVACY?

MY CAMERA...

N...NO...

HA HA HA!

HE DIDN'T DO ANYTHING TO YOU—WHY'D YOU PUSH HIM?

OH, I DIDN'T PUSH HIM. IT WAS MY FRIEND HERE—HE'S REALLY STONED.

WE DIDN'T MEAN TO, HONEST.

THAT'S NOT TRUE—YOU DID IT ON PURPOSE.

AND IT'S WRONG TO FIGHT OUTSIDE THE RING!

HEY, YOU'RE A FEISTY LIL' GUY, AREN'T YA?
SO YOU WANNA FIGHT?
YOU WANNA IMPRESS TOMIE WHEN HER HUSBAND'S NOT AROUND?

HE'S FEISTY TOO!
LEMME INTRODUCE A FRIEND...

...

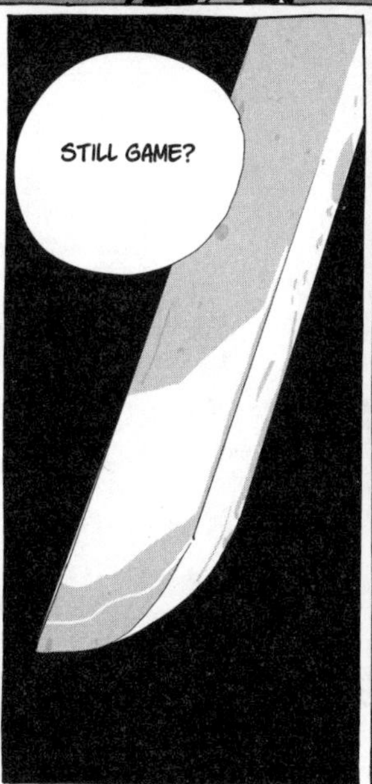
STILL GAME?

NO?
DON'T MOVE, ADRIAN.
VLAM!

WHAT THE...
SERVICE ENTRANCE
NO PARKING
C'MON SWEETIE. LET ME HEAR YOU MAKE SOME PRETTY NOISES IN FRONT OF YOUR LIL' BROTHER...
GET LOST, CREEP.
YOU WANNA TASTE MY BLADE?

WHO THE HELL ARE YOU?
HEH HEH...
WHA—

AAH!
MY HAND!!!
DON'T LOOK!
AAARGH!
CRAASH!

SHA!
CRAAC

WAM!

CRASHH!

DID YOU SEE WHAT HAPPENED?
WITHOUT MY GLASSES, IT WAS ALL A BLUR. TALK ABOUT BAD LUCK!
CRISTO!
ADRIAN!
MY CAMERA!
DO YOU WANT US TO TELL YOUR MOM WHAT HAPPENED?
UM...

NO!
C'MON, ADRIAN, LET'S GET BACK TO THE LOUNGE.
AND HERE. THANKS FOR YOUR HELP.
TOC
TOC
TOC
EVERYTHING OKAY, HONEY?

THINGS WENT WELL?
YUP!
SMAAACK!
TOMIE TAUGHT ME VIDEO GAMES.
THAT SOUNDS GREAT! NOW LET'S GO GET SOME SLEEP.
I'LL CALL YOU A CAB.
GOOD NIGHT!

DOM! DOM! DOM DOM
REST UP FOR TOMORROW!
DOM! DOM!
DOM! DOM!
DOM!

LADIES AND GENTLEMEN!
WELCOME TO THE FINAL PHASE OF THE FIGHT FIST FUNERAL...

...CUUUP!
TONIGHT, YOU'LL BE SEEING THE TOP FIGHTERS GO HEAD-TO-HEAD!
BWHHHHHH!
SO HOLD ON TO YOUR SEATS!
AND NOW, WITHOUT FURTHER ADO... THE FIRST FIGHT!!!

YEAHHHH
TO MY RIGHT, THE TEAM ALL THE LADIES LOVE. THEY'VE GOT BRAWN...
...AND SERIOUS STYLE!
WILLY WHOPPERS!
AND...
TYPHOON TOWERS!
HERE ARE YOUR SEATS.
THANKS, FIONA!
CAN YOU BELIEVE ALL THESE PEOPLE?

GAME ON! WHOPPERS VERSUS NOOB!

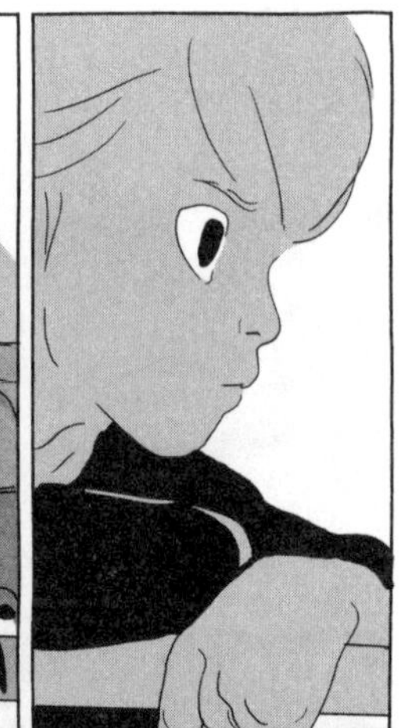

ADRIAN?

WAAAA

WHAT'S WRONG? YOU HAVEN'T BEEN YOURSELF ALL DAY.

OUCH! THAT'S GOTTA HURT!
NOOB IS OFF TO A ROUGH START!

IF YOU EVER WANT TO GO HOME, JUST SAY THE WORD.

I WANT US TO WIN THIS TOURNAMENT.

AND WE WILL. YOU AND ME.
THWACK!

FOR THEIR FIRST SHOWING ON THE BIG STAGE, THIS NEW TEAM IS NOT HAVING AN EASY GO OF IT!
YOU CAN SAY THAT AGAIN! IT'S HIGH TIME FOR NOOB TO HAND OVER TO HIS PARTNER.
STAFF
WHOA! DOUBLE-HEEL KICK!
THUMP
GNN... BILLY.
HE'S TAGGED OUT! BILLY BOSH ENTERS THE FRAY!

AHHH, NICE TRY!
BUT WILLY IS A MASTER AT DEFLECTION.
OW! ELBOW TO THE RIBS!
IT'S NOT LOOKING GOOD FOR BILLY!

WOOOO
BWA
A DOUBLE!
TAP!
TYPHOON
TAKES OVER!
SHPOK

WHAT'S UP, BUDDY?
SHKRANG
...BO!!!
COM...
TYPHOON WINS!!!
AND THE SHOW'S JUST BEGINNING! THE NEXT FIGHT PROMISES TO BE EQUALLY INTENSE...

AFTER SEVERAL YEARS IN HIDING, FOLLOWING A DISASTROUS EXIT THAT ENRAGED HIS FANS–
TO SAY THE LEAST–
A FIGHTER RETURNS WITH HIS MASKED PARTNER...
FFFC
RBC 2V
CRISTO CANY
IT'LL BE INTERESTING TO SEE HOW THE PUBLIC REACTS TO...
RICHARD ALDANA
CRISTO CANY
RICHARD "NO SHAME" ALDANA!
BOOO!
BOOOOOOOOO!
BEER
BOOOOOO!
YOU SUCK!
BOOO!
PAXSTADIUM / CZ
SCREW YOU, ALDANA!
BOOO!
BOOO!

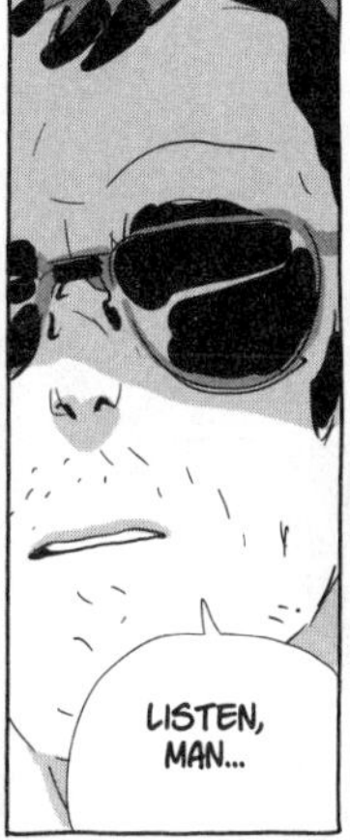
LISTEN, MAN...

I THINK YOU AND I SHOULD TAKE A MINUTE TO TALK.

WHAT I LIKE ABOUT YOU, CRISTO, IS YOU'RE A REAL PRO.
NOW, I DON'T KNOW WHAT MILO PROMISED YOU, BUT THERE ARE PLENTY OF GUYS OUT THERE WHO WANT ME DEAD.

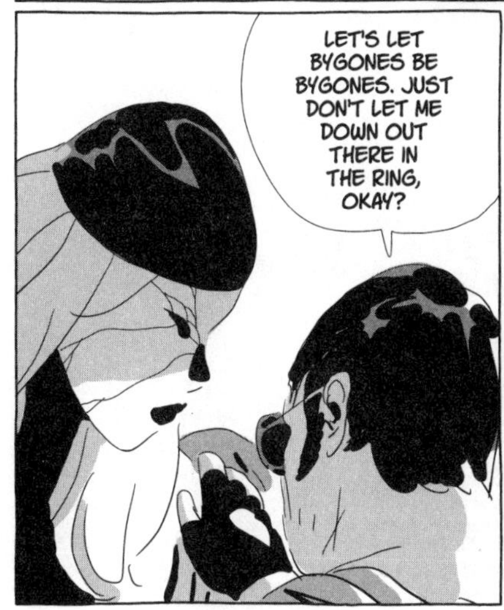
LET'S LET BYGONES BE BYGONES. JUST DON'T LET ME DOWN OUT THERE IN THE RING, OKAY?

ALDANA AND PARTNER– YOU'RE UP!

LADIES AND GENTLEMEN...
PLEASE WELCOME...
RICHARD
"NO SHAME"
ALDANA!!!

WELL, THAT'S QUITE AN OVATION!

SO ARE YOU REALLY SURE ABOUT ALDANA?
HE'S OLD AND FLABBY. CAN HE REALLY MAKE IT TO THE FINAL?

OH, HE'LL BE THERE! YOU CAN ALREADY BOOK YOUR SEAT.

ALDANA WILL MEET HIS END IN FRONT OF A CROWD THAT'S PAID FULL PRICE TO WATCH.
DID YOU PAY OFF HIS OPPONENTS OR SOMETHING?

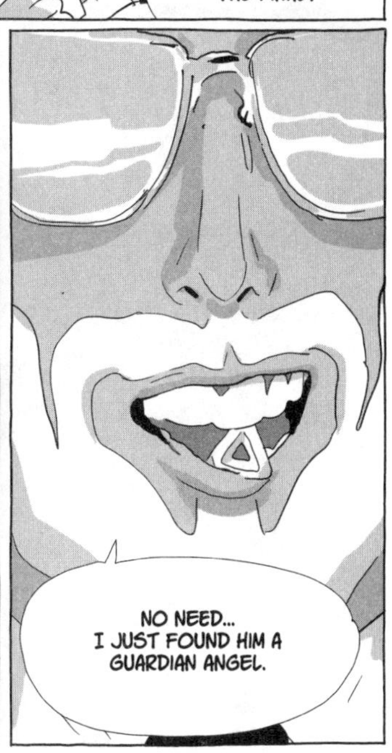
NO NEED... I JUST FOUND HIM A GUARDIAN ANGEL.

WHERE DID YOU FIND HIM, BY THE WAY?
H BROUGHT HIM OVER FROM NILLIPOLIS. YOU WON'T BE DISAPPOINTED.

MARIANNE AND ADRIAN? NO, THEY'RE FROM THE BOONDOCKS– SOME HICK VILLAGE RICHARD WANDERED INTO.

AND THOSE OTHER TWO? ALSO FROM NILLIPOLIS?

HE PULLED THE WOOL OVER THEIR EYES AND MADE OFF WITH THE VILLAGE CUP, THINKING IT COULD PAY HIS DEBT.
RICHARD YOU SUCK
SHAME ON YOU
DOES HE STILL HAVE IT?

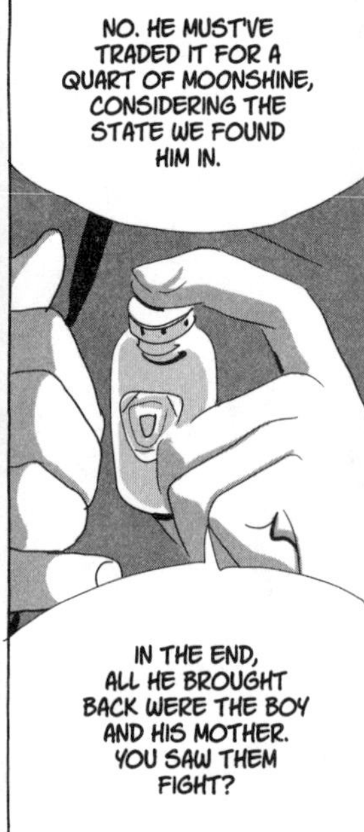
NO. HE MUST'VE TRADED IT FOR A QUART OF MOONSHINE, CONSIDERING THE STATE WE FOUND HIM IN.
IN THE END, ALL HE BROUGHT BACK WERE THE BOY AND HIS MOTHER. YOU SAW THEM FIGHT?

YEAH, I SAW THE REPLAYS ON TV.

YOU SURE THEY'RE NOT "ENHANCED"? WITH SECTOR COMING BACK AND ALL...
IT'S PRETTY UNBELIEVABLE. I DON'T KNOW HOW THEY DO IT.
I DON'T THINK SO. CAN YOU PICTURE THAT MOM SHOOTING UP HER KID? IT'D BE INSANE.

THEY'RE DIAMONDS IN THE ROUGH.

I TOLD YOU WE SHOULDN'T BUMP OFF RICHARD RIGHT AWAY...

HE'S ALWAYS FULL OF SURPRISES!

FFFC SPECIAL
ROUND OF 16
ELBA
RETURN

GOING ALREADY?
YOU'RE GONNA MISS RICHARD'S BOUT.

THAT'S OKAY. IT'S THE NEXT ONE I'M INTERESTED IN.

THE FURYO BROTHERS. TOUGH OPPONENTS.
WAIT TILL YOU SEE CANYON IN THE RING.

ALDANA...

ALDANA MADE IT... HE GOT TO THE VALLEY.

ARE YOU CERTAIN?

JUST ABOUT. MILO HAS NO IDEA WHAT'S AT STAKE. HE WANTS TO GET RID OF ALDANA.

WE NEED HIM ALIVE.

ALDANA'S A LOAD OF CRAP.

I'M FINE WITH MILO KILLING HIM OFF.

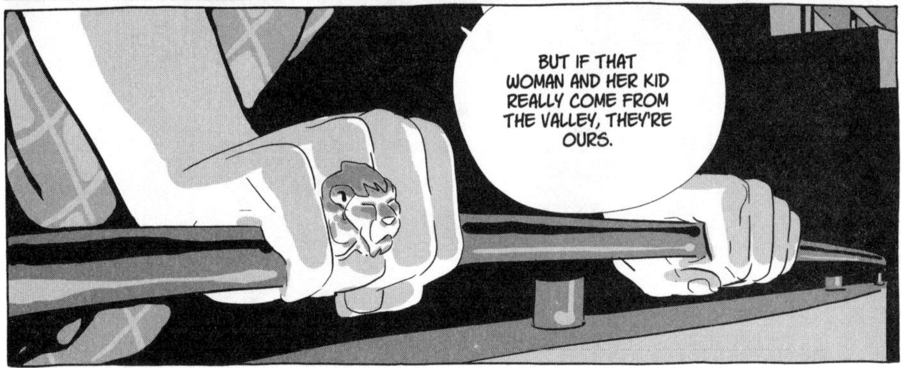

WE'LL HAVE TO ACT SWIFTLY AND DECISIVELY.
WHAT ABOUT THE CUP?

I'M GOING TO INVESTIGATE. ONE THING'S FOR SURE, THOUGH...

IT'S ON THIS SIDE OF THE RIFT.
PAX
TOWN

WE'LL NEED TO CALL UP ALL THE GUARDIANS.

...IS CLOSER THAN WE THINK.

Read on for a preview of

LAST MAN

5

The Order

Balak + Sanlauville + Vivès

Available in July 2016 by First Second Books

ISBN 978-1-62672-050-3

CRR
CRR...

HUH?
SOMETHING'S MOVING.

CAREFUL...
DON'T WORRY, IT'S PROBABLY JUST A LIZARD.

CRR
CRR

I'M NOT SURE THAT'S...

ROAR!!!

KRIII
ROARR!!
?

RRRRRR...
WAIT, THAT'S...
ONI!

THAT'S ADRIAN'S PET.
HE NEARLY RIPPED MY THROAT OUT.
RRR...
HE'S GONE RABID!
IT'S OKAY...
GRRRR.

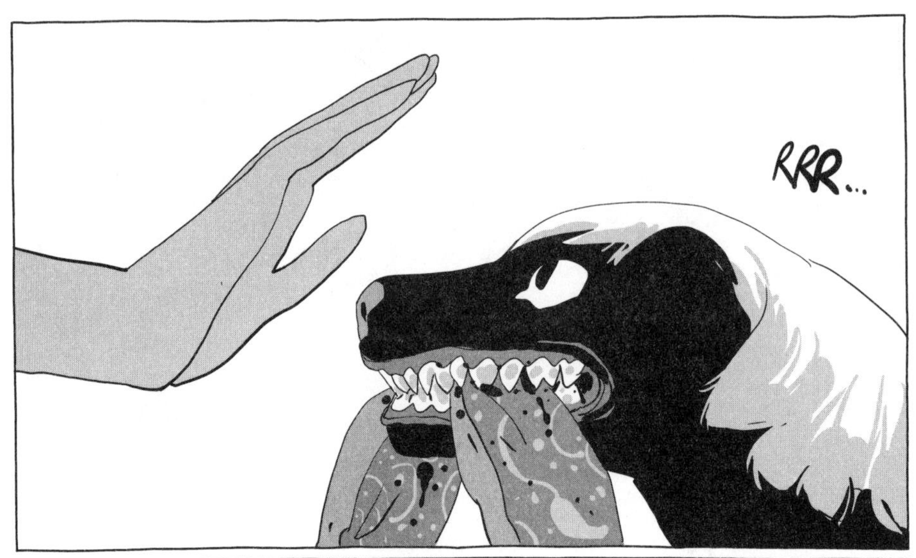
RRR...

ELORNA?

ELORNA!

WHAT DO YOU THINK YOU'RE DOING?
SOMETHING HAPPENED.

THE ETHEREAL FRONTIER...

New York

Published by First Second
First Second is an imprint of Roar
a division of Holtzbrinck Publishi
175 Fifth Avenue, New York, Nev

Library of Congress Cataloging-in

Vivès, Bastien.
[Lastman. 4 English.]
The Show / Bastien Vivès. Mich
American edition.
pages cm. — (Last man ; 4)
ISBN 978-1-62672-049-7 (pape
1. Graphic novels. I Sanlaville, M
PN6747.V58L413 2016
741.5'944—dc23

Our books may be purchased in
or business use. Please contact yo
Corporate and Premium Sales De
or by e-mail at MacmillanSpecial

FIRST
EDITION

Originally published in France by

First American edition 2016

Book design by Rob Steen

Printed in the United States of America

10 9 8 7 6 5 4 3 2 1